Dear Evelyn,

My life is brighter and richer for knowing yo[u] [...] being [...] [Lo]ve,

Carol D.

For a Very Special Person

FOR A 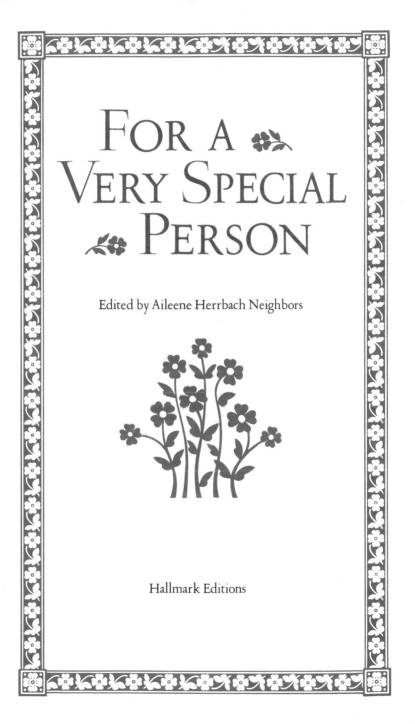 VERY SPECIAL PERSON

Edited by Aileene Herrbach Neighbors

Hallmark Editions

Acknowledgments: "Tribute to a Teacher" taken from *May I Have a Word With You?* by Rabbi Morris Adler. Compiled by Goldie Adler and Lily Edelman. ©1967 by B'nai B'rith. Used by permission of Crown Publishers, Inc. "Finding a Friend" from *The Open Door* by Helen Keller. Copyright ©1957 by Helen Keller. Used by permission of Doubleday & Company, Inc. "Thank-You Note" by Gladys McKee from *Spirit,* A Magazine of Poetry, Seton Hall University, South Orange, New Jersey. Excerpt from *To the Fair Unknown* by André Maurois. Reprinted by permission of Gerald Maurois, Executor of the Estate of André Maurois. "Gratitude" from *Bright Horizons* by Helen Lowrie Marshall. Copyright, 1954, by Helen Lowrie Marshall. Reprinted by arrangement. "Favor" by James J. Metcalfe, author of *Poem Portraits.* Reprinted by permission. Luke 10:30-31, 33-36 from the *Revised Standard Version of the Bible,* copyrighted 1946, 1952, ©1971, 1973. Reprinted by permission of the National Council of the Churches of Christ. "The Mirror of Friendship" by Elizabeth Mauske in the March 1954 *Reader's Digest.* Copyright 1954 by The Reader's Digest Assn., Inc. Lines from "The Kindly Neighbor" reprinted from *The Collected Verse of Edgar Guest,* copyright 1934, 1962, by the Reilly & Lee Company, a division of the Henry Regnery Company, Chicago. "In Favor of Old-Fashioned Grandmothers" by Virginia Brasier from the April 1951 issue of *Today's Health,* published by the American Medical Association. Used with their permission.

For a
Very Special
Person

FAVOR

A favor is that kindly deed...Beyond a friendly smile ...That comforts someone else on earth...And makes this life worthwhile...It may involve a fortune or... The fraction of a cent...Or just some little effort that...Is generously spent...We may be asked to do it or...The thought may be our own...In any case it is the way...Our charity is shown...It is a little sacrifice...That we are glad to make...To brighten up the sky a bit...For someone else's sake...And often we consider it...A privilege to extend...Because there is no greater deed...Than helping out a friend.

James J. Metcalfe

$\int$riendship,
compounded of esteem and love,
derives from one its tenderness
and its permanence from the other.

Samuel Johnson

Friendship
is the golden
thread
that ties
the hearts
of all
the world.

John Evelyn

THE MIRROR
OF FRIENDSHIP

On her frequent trips on foot to Temuco, an old Araucanian Indian woman used always to bring my mother a few partridge eggs or a handful of berries. My mother spoke no Araucanian beyond the greeting "Mai'mai," and the old woman knew no Spanish, but she drank tea and ate cake with many an appreciative giggle. We girls stared fascinated at her layers of colorful hand-woven clothing, her copper bracelets and coin necklaces, and we vied with each other in trying to memorize the singsong phrase she always spoke on rising to leave.

At last we learned the words by heart and repeated them to the missionary, who translated them for us. They have stayed in my mind as the nicest compliment ever uttered: "I shall come again, for I like myself when I'm near you."

Elizabeth Mauske

IN HONOR OF FRIENDSHIP

Two friends lived on adjoining lands—one alone, and the other with his wife and children. They harvested their grain, and one night the man without a family awoke and looked on his sheaves stacked beside him.

"How good God has been to me," he thought, "but my friend with his family needs more grain than I." So he carried some of his store to his friend's field.

And the other, surveying his own harvest, thought: "How much I have to enrich my life. How lonely my friend must be with so little of this world's joys."

So he arose and carried some of his grain and placed it on his friend's stack.

And in the morning when they went forth to glean again, each saw his heap of sheaves undiminished.

The exchange continued until one night in the moonlight the friends met, each with his arms filled on the way to the other's field. At the point where they met, the legend says, *a temple was built.*

Folk Tradition

A friend is a
neighbor of the heart.

Blanche Harris

SPRING MORNING

Life is a spring morning
if you've got a friend,
someone to walk with
and talk with
and turn to.
Life is a spring morning
if you've got a friend
to share a little sun with,
to help you along.
Now and forever...
you've got a friend.

Alan Doan

LITTLE THINGS

It's just the little, homely things,
    The unobtrusive, friendly things,
The "won't-you-let-me-help-you" things
    That make our pathway light—
And it's just the jolly, joking things,
    The "never-mind-the-trouble" things,
The "laugh-with-me, it's-funny" things
    That make the world seem bright.
For all the countless famous things,
    The wondrous, record-breaking things,
Those "never-can-be-equalled" things
    That all the papers cite
Aren't like the little human things,
    The everyday-encountered things,
The "just-because-I-like-you" things
    That make us happy quite.
So here's to all the simple things,
    The dear "all-in-a-day's-work" things,
The "smile-and-face-your-troubles" things.
    Trust God to put them right!
The "done-and-then-forgotten" things,
    The "can't-you-see-I-love-you" things,
The hearty "I-am-with-you" things
    That make life worth the fight.

Author Unknown

My Dear Liszt:

I must say, you are a friend. Let me say more to you, for although I always recognized in friendship between men the noblest and highest relation, it was you who embodied this idea into its fullest reality by letting me no longer imagine, but feel and grasp, what a friend is. I do not thank you, for you alone have the power to thank yourself by your joy in being what you are. It is noble to have a friend, but still nobler to be a friend.

Richard Wagner

WHO IS MY FRIEND?

A man was going down from Jerusalem to Jericho, and he fell among robbers, who stripped him and beat him, and departed, leaving him half dead. Now by chance a priest was going down that road; and when he saw him he passed by on the other side....But a Samaritan, as he journeyed, came to where he was; and when he saw him, he had compassion, and went to him and bound up his wounds, pouring on oil and wine; then he set him on his own beast and brought him to an inn, and took care of him. And the next day he took out two denarii and gave them to the innkeeper, saying, "Take care of him; and whatever more you spend, I will repay you when I come back." Which of these..., do you think, proved neighbor to the man who fell among the robbers?

From the Gospel of St. Luke

True
friendship
foresees
the needs
of others
rather than
proclaims
its own.

André Maurois

IN FAVOR OF
OLD-FASHIONED
GRANDMOTHERS

Grandmother wore great, full, black dresses and a little gold watch on a chain and a black bonnet with sequins and feathers and a bigger black moire dress for Sunday church. But in all that black she never looked severe. She had candy in her workbox and lavender in her handkerchief box....She made us count ten when we got angry at each other, and she fixed us endless slices of bread and butter sprinkled with granulated sugar—despite the fact that Mother thought it bad for our teeth. And Grandmother hid us back of that voluminous skirt, one on either side, when Mother tried to catch us for a scolding. Everyone ended up laughing!

She was fortunate that she owned her own home and sensible enough to refuse any but a short visit to her daughters' who often begged her to come and stay. No wonder everyone wanted her! All her grandchildren, as well as the elders, adored her. Our young adoration, unfortunately, ran to begging for an endless succession of Grimm's fairy tales until her eyes were tired out. But I think the elders loved her because she never criticized any of them. As a matter of fact, she had a good word to say for everyone....

But mine wasn't the only grandmother like this. There were—and are—many such grandmothers....

To children the word has wonderful and delightful meaning: it means someone who loves you but never blames or punishes you....

A grandmother can tell Johnny or Mary to wash his or her hands, or to spend more time reading, or to stand up straight, or not-to-eat-any-more-you'll-be-sick....

A grandmother can spoil and pet and encourage and bind up wounds of the spirit and praise-to-the-skies and be an admiring audience and an infinite lot of other things that mothers are not expected to be. She can do it, not only to her grandchildren, but to her grown-up children too, not to mention a whole host of friends, and even strangers....

So a grandmother must be a harbor of quiet and freedom from blame; a refuge where children can get a straighter and longer view of life as they munch on things that aren't absolutely the best in the world for them....

There is absolutely nothing to take the place of a good, old-fashioned grandmother. She may do a little harm now and then by spoiling her grandchildren, but nothing bad ever came from real love—even an overdose of real love....

Virginia Brasier

Those
who bring
sunshine
to the lives
of others
cannot keep it
from
themselves.

Sir James Barrie

I'LL ALWAYS REMEMBER...

Helen was my mother's best friend; but in many ways, I think she was one of my best friends, too. She always treated me as though I really knew what I was doing, even if I didn't! I remember the summer I decided to grow a whole garden of vegetables. "Fresh salads for everyone," I dreamed. I struggled with the spading and planting and hoeing; and I must admit that for a while my patch looked pretty dismal. But Helen always believed I would succeed. I'll never forget the day she asked me—confidential like—if she could have some tomatoes when they came up.

"How I love tomatoes," she said. Now that showed confidence just when I needed it most. Even today, when I'm working on a difficult project or encounter some problem, I think of Helen and her help that summer. Those thoughts are always like a breath of new life.   'Tina Hacker

The glow of one warm thought
        is to me worth more than money.

Thomas Jefferson

To hear the whispered voice
of another's heart
and understand unspoken words
are talents of those lucky few—
people who are precious to the world.

Theresa Ann Hunt

SMALL SERVICE

Small service is true service while it lasts;
Of friends, however humble, scorn not one;
The daisy by the shadow that it casts
Protects the lingering dew-drop from the sun.

William Wordsworth

SUNSHINE AND MUSIC

A laugh is just like sunshine.
It freshens all the day,
It tips the peak of life with light
And drives the clouds away.
The soul grows glad that hears it
And feels its courage strong.
A laugh is just like sunshine
For cheering folks along.

A laugh is just like music.
It lingers in the heart,
And where its melody is heard
The ills of life depart;
And happy thoughts come crowding,
Its joyful notes to greet:
A laugh is just like music
For making living sweet.

Author Unknown

No one is rich enough
        to do without a neighbor.

Danish Proverb

From THE KINDLY NEIGHBOR

I have a kindly neighbor, one who stands
Beside my gate and chats with me awhile,
Gives me the glory of his radiant smile
And comes at times to help with willing hands.
No station high or rank this man commands;
He, too, must trudge, as I, the long day's mile;
And yet, devoid of pomp or gaudy style,
He has a worth exceeding stocks or lands.

To him I go when sorrow's at my door;
On him I lean when burdens come my way;
Together oft we talk our trials o'er,
And there is warmth in each good-night we say.
A kindly neighbor! Wars and strife shall end
When man has made the man next door his friend.

Edgar A. Guest

A SISTER

A sister is a wonderful girl
Who's full of things to be done.
She delights and amuses her family
With all kinds of surprises and fun.
Yes, a sister's a wonderful female,
It's a joy to have her around,
And when you need understanding,
No better friend can be found.
And when a sister is older,
With each passing year you'll find
She's always a good companion—
The sweetest and loveliest kind!

Barbara Burrow

THE ROAD IS BEFORE US

Allons! the road is before us!

It is safe—I have tried it—my own feet have tried it
    well—be not detain'd!
Let the paper remain on the desk unwritten, and the
    book on the shelf unopen'd!

Let the tools remain in the workshop! let the money
    remain unearn'd!
Let the school stand! mind not the cry of the teacher!
Let the preacher preach in his pulpit! let the lawyer
    plead in the court, and the judge expound the law.

Camerado, I give you my hand!
I give you my love more precious than money,
I give you myself before preaching or law;
Will you give me yourself? will you come travel with me?
Shall we stick by each other as long as we live?

               Walt Whitman

After the verb
to love,
to help is the most
beautiful
verb
in the world!

Countess Bertha von Suttner

LOVING FLOWERS
AND SPECIAL MEMORIES

Albert was a man who loved flowers. Now other people may scoff at the opinion that plants have emotions, but not Albert. He knew it for a fact. He was a gardener at the college I attended, and I do believe he had an intimate friendship with just about every tree, shrub, bush and flower on campus. No matter how scraggly or scruffy a plant might appear, Albert could make it better.

He especially liked to tend the rose garden near my dorm. As my friends and I would walk to class, he'd chide us about taking better care of our potted plants—good naturedly, of course. And by and by, we all came to look forward to his cheery hello and helpful words of advice. Albert always knew exactly how to care for a wilted philodendron or sagging ivy. No matter how busy he was, he would have the time to chat or to listen to a problem. It didn't take long before each of us in the dorm felt that this man who was every plant's best friend was our friend, too.

I recall a day near graduation time when I was sitting on the dorm porch, my head filled with memories of the good times I had enjoyed on campus—the parties and debates over cokes, the late-night pizzas and the comraderies made in four years. Albert happened to come by just then and, noticing me, stopped to visit for a few minutes—or so I thought. What he had to say was not, "How's economics coming along?" or, "Have you heard about that job you applied for?" Instead, he said he had a graduation present especially for me. There in the garden, Albert pointed to my present—a rose bush in full bloom. "It's all yours," he exclaimed.

"Mine?" I said, puzzled. "You're not going to dig it up, are you?" Uprooting a plant, to Albert, was a sacrilege.

"Oh, no," he continued. "But I told this very plant that it belonged to a special lady. She was going to be leaving this place soon, but would be back to visit from time to time. I hear roses mean remembering, and I guess, maybe, they do."

"Yes, Albert, they do," I thought. And although I suspected every girl who was graduating that year received "her" rose bush for a gift, I couldn't help but feel that somehow it was really mine.

It's been a few years now since I left school, but every spring I go back to campus for a visit to see old friends, teachers, my rose bush and Albert. He was right. The roses have helped me to remember time and time again how a man who loved flowers made that campus a very happy place.

Tina Hacker

ON LIFE

What seems to grow fairer
to me as life goes by
is the love and the grace
and tenderness of it;
not its wit and cleverness
and grandeur
of knowledge—
grand as knowledge is—
but just the laughter
of children
and the friendship
of friends,
and the cosy talk
by the fire,
and the sight of flowers,
and the sound of music.

Eleanor Leah Woods

FRIENDSHIP

Friendship is a chain of gold
Shaped in God's all perfect mold,
Each link a smile, a laugh, a tear,
A touch of the hand, a word of cheer.

Author Unknown

 friend is one who:
    pushes you in the swing,
      pulls you up the ladder,
        pats you on the back
          and hugs you good-bye.

Katherine N. Davis

A FRIEND IN NEED

"A friend in need," my neighbor said to me,
"A friend indeed is what I mean to be;
In time of trouble I will come to you,
And in the hour of need you'll find me true."

I thought a bit, and took him by the hand:
"My friend," said I, "you do not understand
The inner meaning of that simple rhyme;
A friend is what the heart needs all the time."

Henry van Dyke

Blessed are they who have the gift of making friends, for it is one of God's best gifts. It involves many things, but above all, the power of going out of one's self, and appreciating whatever is noble and loving in another.

Thomas Hughes

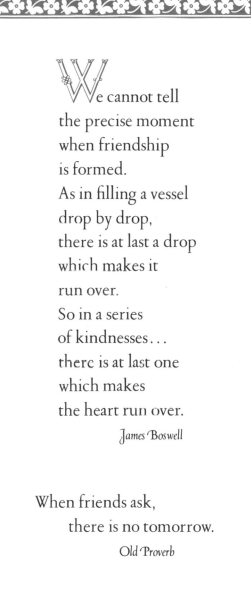

We cannot tell
the precise moment
when friendship
is formed.
As in filling a vessel
drop by drop,
there is at last a drop
which makes it
run over.
So in a series
of kindnesses...
there is at last one
which makes
the heart run over.

James Boswell

When friends ask,
    there is no tomorrow.

Old Proverb

When the world
seems large and complex,
we need to remember
that great world ideals
all begin in some
home neighborhood.

Konrad Adenauer

GENEROSITY

All hearts grow warmer in the presence
Of one who, seeking not his own,
Gave freely for the love of giving,
Nor reaped for self the harvest sown.
Thy greeting smile was pledge and prelude
Of generous deeds and kindly words,
In thy large heart were fair guest-chambers,
Open to sunrise and the birds.

John Greenleaf Whittier

THE HEROISM
OF THE MOTHER

Is not the highest heroism that which is free even from the approbation of the best and wisest? The heroism which is known only to our Father, who seeth in secret? The God-like lives lived in obscurity? How many thousands of heroines there must be now, of whom we shall never know. But still they are there. They sow in secret the seed of which we pluck the flower, and eat the fruit, and know not that we pass the sower daily in the streets.

One form of heroism—the most common, and yet the least remembered of all—namely, the heroism of the average mother. Ah! When I think of that broad fact, I gather hope again for poor humanity; and this dark world looks bright—this diseased world looks wholesome to me once more—because, whatever else it is not full of, it is at least full of mothers.

Charles Kingsley

Dear Hank,

Surprise! A letter from your wife! So many things get left unsaid from day to day—I had to tell you right this minute how I'm feeling about you. About us.

Do you know how glad I am that you're my lover and pal and partner, too? In fact, you're my best friend. We never seem to run out of things to talk about and do. Sometimes, we simply enjoy leaning against that warm cushion of silence between us. Either way, you always seem to know the mood I'm in.

When you get right down to it, we're two very different people. But maybe that's what makes you so interesting to me every day.

Here's a kiss on the nose for being you. My mind will hold you close all day. Wish you could come home early!

All my love,

Janine

TO FRIENDSHIP

A friend is someone lovely who
Cuts her chrysanthemums for you
And, giving, cares not for the cost,
Nor sees the blossoms she has lost;
But, rather, values friendship's store
Gives you her best
         and grows some more.

Eleanor Long

The language of friendship
    is not words but meanings.

Henry David Thoreau

FINDING A FRIEND

There are red-letter days in our lives when we meet people who thrill us like a fine poem, people whose handshake is brimful of unspoken sympathy, and whose sweet, rich natures impart to our eager, impatient spirits a wonderful restfulness which, in its essence, is divine.

The perplexities, irritations, and worries that have absorbed us pass like unpleasant dreams, and we wake to see with new eyes and hear with new ears the beauty and harmony of God's real world.

Helen Keller

Loving - kindness
is greater
than laws;
and the charities
of life
are more than
all ceremonies.

The Talmud

REV. HARRY L. THOMAS

Rev. Harry L. Thomas never talked down to us kids,
no matter how silly we acted. I blush when I think of
the outrageous questions we asked—just to bait him a
little. He'd smile gently and answer us with sincerity,
wisdom and, above all, patience. So we'd learn some-
thing in spite of ourselves. We loved him like a father
and he, in turn, taught us to love our Father above.

Robin St. John

Some people
    make the world brighter
        just by being in it.

Mary Dawson Hughes

GRATITUDE

"How can I ever repay you?"
I've said it, and so have you.
How can I ever in all this world
Repay the things you do?

Perhaps I never can repay
To you—or you to me,
But we can pass that kindness on
To others we may see.

And though you never need my help—
I pray you never do—
By helping others, I'll repay
My heartfelt debt to you.

Helen Lowrie Marshall.

THANK YOU

A tiny bouquet of fresh cut flowers
can fill a room with sunshine.
A little act of kindness
can fill a heart with joy.

Katherine Nelson

Nature produced us related to one another, since she created us from the same source and to the same end. She engendered in us mutual affection and made us prone to friendships .... Through her orders, our hands are ready to help in the good work. Our relations with one another are like a stone arch, which would collapse if the stones did not mutually support each other, and which is upheld in this very way.

Seneca

A DAD KNOWS

A dad knows how to give
his children good advice.
But he also knows
that his children need
to think things out
for themselves and form
their own conclusions.
There are times when
they must do the talking,
times when they can
really use a friend
who will just listen...
and understand.

Edward Cunningham

IT'S FRIENDSHIP

It's as old as man himself,
    yet as new as this moment or the next.
It's ever changing
    and somehow ever constant.
It's stronger
    than any wall ever built.
It overcomes politics
    and national barriers.
It can't be blinded by strange customs
    or blocked by foreign languages.
It has been written about
    and analyzed by wise men;
Yet it has never been defined,
    and never will be.
You can't see it or touch it;
    yet it is everywhere.

It survives weakness and neglect,
   thrives on thoughtfulness.
Its possibilities are infinite;
   its strength limitless.
It's what makes man human,
   what makes life worth living.
It's friendship.

Eleanor Leah Woods

TRIBUTE TO A TEACHER

He was a teacher—this was the first and most vivid impression he gave. He was one whose personality did not contract into his profession, but on the contrary his calling, for it was more than an occupational pursuit, broadened and streamed into his entire being.

He was a teacher, and therefore his was a poetic sensitivity to growth, to enlargement. Only a poet hears the grass grow, witnesses the flowers in their actual blossoming, beholds the ripening in process in field and meadow. And only a teacher actually sees the seedlings of the youthful mind reaching out for the light, germinating and sprouting under the loving touch of an inspired gardener.

He was a teacher and therefore a creative artist working in the most precious and intricate of all media—the human complex of mind and heart and conscience. To mold and to evoke, to guide and to ignite, and yet not to trespass upon the inner integrity and individuality of the child—this was the incredibly difficult and significant task upon which he was set.

He was a teacher and therefore one who is forever bent on the greatest adventure of all, the exploration of another's mind, the delving into another spirit to mine, uncover and bring forth into the light the possibilities that lie hidden in the deeps. No diver descended into the sea in search of treasure, no explorer journeyed to unknown continents with greater anticipation and higher excitement.

He was a teacher, and therefore he loved his fellowman. Neither his skill nor his diligence were substituted for the love which led him to devote himself to the instruction of his neighbor and his neighbor's child.

He was a teacher and therefore one who revered the word, honored ideas, exalted thought and fostered the great dream. He was a teacher and knew with conviction that the hope of men lies not in their machines or in their power or in their uncultivated ego but in the refinement, mutuality and sensitivity which the thinker, poet, saint and dreamer awaken in them. He sought to redeem men, not by enlarging their mastery over the outer world but by cultivating their inner universe.

Rabbi Morris Adler

THANK-YOU NOTE

It was one of those days cast in gray,
Sky and heart and the feel of the day,
And nothing minted of earth or strange
And precious fabric could make it change
Until you sent me a loaf of bread
You made yourself. I saw your head
Over a blue bowl, over a book
Reading the recipe, love in your look,
Strength in your fingers, and your heart
Yielding the secret, golden part
That makes this more than fine spun wheat,
That makes the heart and the gray day sweet,
With the curious leaven one can blend
In a golden loaf of bread for a friend.

Gladys McKee

Set in Romanee, a twentieth-century typeface designed by Jan van Krimpen of Holland. Designed by Lilian Weytjens.